THE
Archive Photographs
SERIES

HYDE

THE SECOND SELECTION

Mothers and children from Werneth Avenue, Shaw Avenue, Allen Avenue and Mottram Old Road, gathered together to celebrate VE Day in 1945.

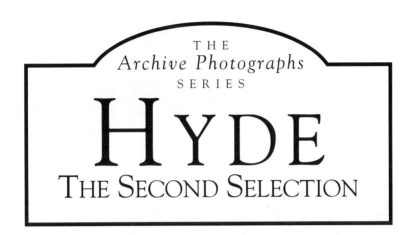

THE
Archive Photographs
SERIES

HYDE

THE SECOND SELECTION

Compiled by
Barbara Sole

CHALFORD

First published 1998
Copyright © Barbara Sole, 1998

The Chalford Publishing Company
St Mary's Mill, Chalford,
Stroud, Gloucestershire, GL6 8NX

ISBN 0 75241033 4

Typesetting and origination by
The Chalford Publishing Company
Printed in Great Britain by
Bailey Print, Dursley, Gloucestershire

Festival Queen. Back row, from left to right: -?-, Mr Mansfield, -?-, Miss J. West, -?-, Mr Dakin. Seated on the left is Dorothy Wilson and on the right, Alwyn Smith.

Contents

Acknowledgements

Alma Adams, Kathleen Adams, Automasters, Mrs Barton, Steve Cliffe, Jim and Joan Coggins, Joyce Crighton, William Cullen, Denton Historical Society, Mr and Mrs D. Dyson, Mr and Mrs David Garrett, Mr and Mrs Greaves, Trevor Grimshaw, Mr and Mrs Hallas, Alwyn Hill, Hyde Historical Society, Susan Jaleel, Jim Kerfoot, Harry Lever, Barry and Linda Lewis, Bill and Nell Lewis, Raymond Masser, Mrs P. Paterson, Edith Pimlott, Mr and Mrs Michael Reed, Mrs D. Robinson, Edith Robinson, Neville Robinson, John Slater, Cathleen Smith, Charles Smith, Barbara Sole, Alan and Brenda Taylor, Werneth Country Park, Brenda Wigley.

The author would like to offer apologies to anyone who has not been included in these acknowledgements. I have relied entirely on contributers to provide the names of individuals and also part of the text. Apologies are also offered to anyone whose name has been spelt incorrectly or who has been wrongly identified.

This book is dedicated to the people of Hyde, wherever they may be.

Introduction

The introduction to my first book followed the growth of Hyde from AD 383 into the 1960s. This volume pursues its history into the 1980s. During the last forty years there have been many changes in the buildings, the shopping areas, the market, the population and local government.

In the 1930s when the population was 33,000, Hyde was a very busy industrial town within easy reach of the countryside. It was a very proud town which had its own mayor and councillors - people you could easily approach with any problem. This state of affairs continued until 1974 but from this time local government has been administered by Ashton. These administrative and physical changes cannot take away our 'living memories' nor our written histories, but they tend to make us reflect more.

At one time Hyde was a very closely knit community where everyone knew most people's names or nicknames. Employment opportunities here and abroad have enticed many a Hydonian away from the area, though many revisit the town.

Many family shops have disappeared due to the arrival of the 'multiples'. Businesses that have employed the people of Hyde for many years have either closed (Redfern's Rubber Works Ltd, 1985), are due to close (Senior Service), or are moving premises (John North's Complex).

Entertainment has changed drastically. Before the First World War sensation seekers would flock to Hyde to see freak shows such as *Leonine the Lion Faced Lady* and *Alice Bounds the Bear Lady*. In later years the picture palaces, the Astoria, the Star, the Hippodrome, the Queen's, the Ritz and the Theatre Royal provided good family entertainment. In the Town Hall concerts and dances were held along with festivals and bazaars. Many churches and schools would frequently hold concerts by their choirs and drama groups and there were many dance classes in the area. Other groups gathered to play football, cricket, snooker and darts. There were the Boys Brigade, Girl Guides, Youth Clubs, Scouts, Campaigners and the Salvation Army. The progress over the last fifty years in electronics has been, to some extent, one of the major influences in moulding the way in which we now spend out leisure time.

Not only has science brought about changes; wars have also played their part, along with the growth of the population. Many improvements in homes have taken place. Semi-detached and detached houses separate neighbours by gardens; flats by height and walls. People have had to move more to the perimeter of the town, old homes have been demolished. However, we have had some environmental improvements. Many old buildings and bridges have been cleaned, bringing back their former lustre. The old community has been split in many ways but there is still a deep sense of belonging.

Every year at Whitsuntide the congregation of each church would gather together to walk round their parish to celebrate their belief in God. Later all the churches would assemble in the Market Square in front of the Town Hall and unite in a joint celebratory service. This was enacted for ninety years until 1985 and the tradition is sadly missed by many of the inhabitants.

Some of the rural aspects have not changed, especially Werneth Low. This was due to alter but was saved by the Hyde Action Group. If they had not spoken up, the developers would have moved in and the Country Park would not exist for the young people of Hyde to enjoy.

Change I suppose, is inevitable, but let us make sure that the change is for the best.

I came here as a Mancunian thirty years ago. My roots are now in Gee Cross, where I aim to stay.

One
Rural Scenes

Mottram Old Road, 1905. In the foreground is Apple Street winding its way down to the Old Road. A little to the right is Rhodes Farm Fold. To the extreme right is the silhouette of Mottram Church. The people on the left would probably be returning from their Sunday walk along Mottram Old Road, which was known locally as the 'Promenade'.

Haymaking, Werneth Low, 1905. Friends and families were always there to lend a hand. The lady on the left, dressed in all her finery, along with the child on the left, is definitely not part of the haymaking team.

A sports day on Werneth Low, c. 1905. Whether they were roped off while watching a race or about to participate in a tug of war is not known. The young lads are all sporting their caps and the girls their bonnets. The Union Jack is flying in the centre so possibly it was Empire Day. The tower on the right may be Wright's Tower.

There are many springs and wells on the Low and in the surrounding villages. It was around these springs and wells that homes and workshops were built. Most of them have names such as Booth's Well, near the Grapes Hotel and Joel's Well, half way up Joel Lane. At one time well dressing took place and the wells were adorned with flowers; at the Grapes Hotel there was a peacock design flanking the doorway and festoons of evergreens and flowers were thrown across the streets, accompanied by mottoes such as 'Welcome friends' and 'Success to the springs may they never run dry'. People came from far and near for the occasion.

Higher Higham Farm. Situated on Werneth since the late 1500s, it is built of irregular, coarse dressed stone. Many alterations have been carried out as can be seen by the blocked doorway to the left, with the wooden lintel showing. Opposite the farm is a well named the Gin Well. Presumably the water was very clear. The court records from Werneth Manor still exist. They state that in 1588-1658 the occupants had the right to crops and to maintain the farm buildings. However there is a break in the records from 1640 to 1657, during which time it seems that the farm was enlarged by the purchase of the adjoining lands from Reginald Thornley and Thomas Hyde without the permission of the lord of the manor.

Cock Brow. Windy Harbour Farm was on the site opposite Harbour Lights on the Low. It had stone mullion windows and oak roof beams that slotted together like a jigsaw. The thick timber was in perfect condition and many of the beams were virtually tree trunks; in fact, some still had their bark from the day they were cut about 300 years ago. A Mr Hodgekinson farmed there at one time, the great, great grandfather of Miss Alma Adams. Possibly built between 1650 and 1700, it was eventually turned into a shippon and later still, into the Windy Harbour Professional Golf Club shop.

In 1988 the stone roof and the beams were sold for conservation purposes in the Macclesfield area and the stone from the walls was used to refurbish the walls in the park.

At one time Lower Higham Farm operated quite successfully as a working farm. Here is Harry Jackson, who was one of the tenants, with his dog *Teddy* standing outside the granary steps in 1934.

As the years went by it ceased to be a farm and became derelict.

Now the farm has been renovated and turned into Werneth Country Park which consists of 200 acres, three quarters of which belong to the Hyde War Memorial Trust. The park caters for every age, promoting conservation as well as providing many planned walks.

The site of a disused quarry at the top of Joel Lane, 1970. It is now a car park.

Werneth Low is a drumlin, a hill from which one can view the surrounding towns such as Manchester, Oldham, Rochdale, Ashton, Stalybridge, Mottram, Marple and Stockport. When visibility is good Winter Hill and the Welsh hills can be seen. The 54 acres of land were bought with money raised by the people of Hyde after the First World War. Every week their pennies and halfpennies were collected and over £14,000 was raised. £4,000 purchased Lower Higham Farm and the estate; £2,000 was used to build the memorial. This was composed of grey Cornish granite taken from the same quarries as those used for the Cenotaph in London. On the front is the borough's coat of arms in bronze then, travelling clockwise, the following inscriptions appear: 'They willingly left the unachieved purpose of their lives in order that a life should not be wrenched from its purpose'. 'In honour of the 710 men of Hyde who gave their lives for King and Country.' 'In memory of the men and women of Hyde who lost their lives in the war 1939-1945'. The obelisk was unveiled on 25 June 1921. Each year there are two ceremonies held here, on Peace Day in June and Remembrance Sunday in November.

In 1968 Queen Elizabeth II came to Hyde to celebrate Operation Spring Clean. Her Majesty planted three sycamore trees in the triangle of greenery on the Low. The stone below the trees reads, 'This sycamore was planted by the Queen on the occasion of her visit to view Operation Spring Clean on 16 May 1968'. During April 1982 it was suggested that at this point on the Low there could be mysterious forces of elemental electricity energy being charged through invisible tracks criss-crossing the area, namely Ley lines.

Hibbert's field at the bottom of the Low (now Queens Drive). Here there was once a market garden run by George and Dicky Taylor. The children in the picture are Noel Harrison on the right and Alf Harrison on the left.

16

Two
Homes and Buildings

A view across the roof tops of Hyde in 1983. To the left is Grundy House, to the centre the Town Hall. To the right of the Town Hall is the gasometer, then the Co-op and the back of the shops in Market Place; the dome to the extreme right is Woolworth's.

A sudden afternoon cloud burst in May 1906 caused flash floods in the Hyde area. This is Higham Lane after the flood subsided. In less than 1 hour there was 5 inches of rain. Water poured down the hillside ripping up roads as it went. The children of Holy Trinity School (centre) had to cross the road via a plank of wood with the help of a local policeman called Robert.

Godley Brook during the flood of 1906, two minutes before the bridge collapsed.

Treacle Brew in Gee Cross. This leads from Mottram Old Road to the Werneth Hotel on Stockport Road. Stories abound about this cobbled path, one being of an uncontrolled horse and cart descending the Brew and supposedly going straight across Stockport Road into the hollow where there was once a large pond. The horse and cart sank and were never seen again.

The ornate bus shelter opposite the Town Hall on Market Street. Many people think it is Victorian but on many old photographs of the Town Hall and Market Place taken in the early 1900s, the shelter is not there.

Close to where the 'Big Tree' was in Gee Cross there is now a war memorial on the parkland created out of the Diamond Reservoir. It was dedicated by Earl Kitchener of Khartoum TDDL, who was the Cheshire County President of the Royal British Legion. A tree was planted and on the commemorative stone it appropriately states, 'Big Tree', remembering sacrifices made in Northern Ireland and the Falklands Conflict. The date was St George's Day, 23 April 1983.

This 40 ft long, 8 ft wide and 7 ft deep tunnel was exposed during the building of the Village Hotel Squash Club. It is thought that it might have been a draught chamber for Hyde Junction Dye Works.

In 1976 the M67 was constructed to ease the traffic problems in Hyde, changing much of the topography. This view was taken before the rerouting of the Peak Canal at the side of Automasters.

This shows the land cleared between Ashton Brothers and Commercial Brow during the construction of the by-pass.

The Parsonage on Apethorn Lane, Gee Cross, 1920s. This was the residence of the ministers of Hyde Chapel, the most notable one being the Reverend Enfield Dowson. Sadly it was pulled down in 1973.

Gerrards on Stockport Road, Gee Cross. The tower in the middle had a clock face on each side to enable the workers to get to work on time. Inscribed on the clock were the words 'While thou lookest, I fly'. It was built by Thomas Ashton.

Dowson Road, Gee Cross.

Dowson Road was built in 1923 and named after Revd Enfield Dowson, who watched it being constructed from his sitting room window in the Parsonage. By the 1930s homes had been built along one side and facing them were fields leading down to the Peak Forest Canal and the River Tame.

Dowson Road, Gee Cross.

Dowson Road with Apethorn Lane to the left and Stockport Road to the right. Also on the left is an old concrete design of an early GPO telephone kiosk. In the centre a single decker bus is on its way to Stockport. To the extreme right are Hyde Chapel and Enfield Street School. Note the tram lines and cobbled road.

An expanse of roof tops at Hyde, taken in the 1950s from the top of the chimney which was at James North's. Hyde Town Hall is to the far left, then Senior Service (Hyde Mill). Two thirds down on the left is the recreation ground in Douglas Street, Queen Street Mill is in the centre and to the right of that is a reservoir.

Woodfield House, at the bottom of Knott Lane, was built in 1844 when the rateable value was £42 17s 6d (£42 92.5p) The area was once known as 'Little England'. The land was owned by a Daniel Wood who also owned Knott Fold estate. The tenants of the house in 1844 were William Kemp; in 1846 Joseph Redfern lived there, in 1849 Thomas Howard and in 1850, John Wilde. Behind the house were five cottages.

Dingle Cottage on Stockport Road, Gee Cross.

This row of cottages opposite the Lamb Inn on Stockport Road, Gee Cross, is known locally as 'Jolly Bant Row'. It was constructed from stone which had once been the fabric of a mill. In the early days Gee Cross was more important than Hyde because it had plenty of water to develop its mills. On the side of the stream which once flowed from Werneth Low down to the River Tame, there were five cotton mills. After steam power was introduced Hyde took precedence due to the plentiful supply of coal there and the mills at Gee Cross closed. So one enterprising man used the stone, which was of course already dressed and cut, to build this row of houses.

Weaver's cottages on Mottram Old Road. At one time this part of Mottram Old Road was named Treacle Hill. These cottages have two storeys at the front and three at the back.

Gee Cross village, 1905. On the left is the post office before it was altered by the local council who wanted to widen School Lane to enable the trams to go down. They changed the post office but the rest of the plan did not come to fruition. The next shops consisted of Armitage the cloggers and a shop which sold oil for lamps. In the winter when the ponds froze over children inevitably wanted to skate, but many of them could not afford skates so the clogger would fit irons onto their clogs. Next is the Queen's Mill, then the Queen Adelaide pub and just beyond that, the Methodist Church. There is a double decker tram coming up from Hyde and a milk cart in front. The building protruding on the right would be the old police station. This card was sent to Mr W. Woolley, c/o Mrs Gibbson, Druggist, Madoc Street, Llandudno. The message on the back was, 'Puzzle, find Mary Jane Mottram, you will have to look closely', signed 'G.C.' and dated 25 April 1905 at 9.00 pm. The lady in question is just by Queen's Mill.

Stockport Road, Gee Cross, looking towards Gerrards. On the right behind the trees is Spout House Farm. In the centre is a tram on its way to Stockport.

Rose Hannah Lowe at the front door of her home in Foundry Street, dressed in her crocheted waistcoat, sleeves rolled up for some chore and wearing clogs with iron tips on her feet.

Shawcross Street, off Mottram Old Road. This house has had its fair share of ghostly visits: a young girl in a blue dress weeping, footsteps, noises, the rattling of a coal scuttle, a man named Jonathan, the smell of tobacco and a cat.

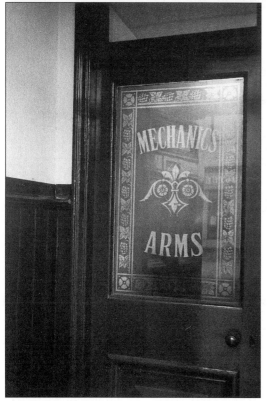

The old doorway of the Mechanics Arms which was on Clarendon Place. It was built in the 1830s and closed in 1921. The first licensee was a Mr John Reynolds who remained there until 1850.

The flying bomb *blitz* at Hyde on 24 December 1944 at 6.30 am. The rescue service was called to Westwood Farm off Mottram New Road. The team consisted of T. Robinson, A. Ashton, E. Kinder, N. Harrison, H. Grey, J. Jones, J. Brookes and T. Harrison. Two persons were freed, both deceased, one male aged about 18 and a female aged about 60. The certificate was issued on site by Dr Ellis of Hyde. Another male was found trapped by debris in his bed. The dead young male was well nourished and adequately clothed and believed to be one Gordon Faulkes; the female was believed to be his grandmother. The bodies were removed to a temporary mortuary at the New Inn and the rescue team also assisted in the recovery of cattle from the debris of the shippon. Two were dead and four were destroyed humanely.

Outside the Queen Adelaide in the 1940s. The man with the panama hat is Bill Emery. Most of the men are sporting a carnation in their lapels. The landlord Tom Booth is standing in the doorway with his wife, the only lady present. It was probably the beginning of a day's outing for the men.

Hallbottom Street, Newton. Hallbottom Chapel was built in 1820, just opposite where Garden Street playing fields are now. The field was once a valley where the cemetery to the chapel was located. In 1934 it was decided to fill in the valley so the graves had to be cleared and the occupants reburied. This was done during the night by lamplight to avoid upsetting people. During the excavation they found one corpse rolled in an animal hide; it was a man who had hung himself. Suicides were not buried in consecrated ground nor would anybody make a coffin for them. Their remains were taken to Hyde Cemetery where a communal grave was dug and a memorial stone erected.

St George's lych gate. The wood to build this gate was thought to have come from Syddal Fold Farm which had been in the area from 1669-1884. It was erected by Thomas Ferns, Handford Fern and Lee Hyde in 1885. Their names were carved on the eaves beam. The hammered dressed stone walls carried the slate roof on wooden posts.

This crypt once stood in all its glory in St Paul's Church grounds in Godley.

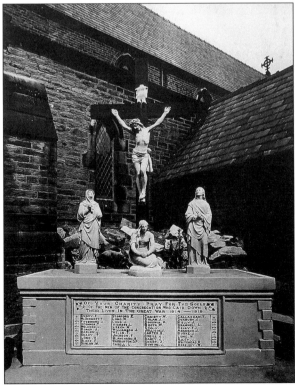

The war memorial that stood in the grounds of St Paul's Church, Godley.

The fourth enlargement to Hyde Chapel, Gee Cross, the foundation day of which was in October 1985. Resplendent in their red and black uniforms, Adamson's Military Band played for the procession of the minister the Reverend Angus McCormick, the Rose Queen Lisa Shufflebottom, the May Queen Alison Hill, trustee's chairman Mr T. Hatton, secretary Mr J.C. Byle, treasurer Mr George Barker and Leonard J. Hulse, whose duty was to lay the foundation stone.

The Primitive Methodist Church was situated at the bottom of Joel Lane in Gee Cross. It was opened in February 1876 and closed in the late 1960s. At one time it had its own little school, just like the other local churches.

This tablet reads 'To the young men of this church (Primitive Methodist) and Sunday School, who responded to Britain's call at the crisis of a great national period. The following paid the extreme sacrifice: Thomas Sampson, Fred Robbins, Joseph J. Wardle, Herbert Belsford, Harold W. Wardle and John H. Walsh'.

In the 1850s Gee Cross was a thriving community but there was no church for Church of England worshippers. They had to travel to the Parish Church of Werneth, St Paul's at Compstall. A room was hired by a Mr Bradley for Anglican worship; in 1858 land was given by Mr Tatton of Wythenshawe and a church combined with a school was erected. The three largest rooms were used as a church and the two smaller ones as the school. On this picture of Holy Trinity School one can see the old church windows.

The end of an era: Gee Cross Mill, 1987.

'Owd Joss', the Town Hall clock. Joshua Bradley (1817-1898) from Godley took great pride in the town of Hyde. He started work as a piecer at Pudding Lane Thread Manufacturers and through hard work rose to become the manager of Boston Mill. He presented the bells for the clock in 1884. The clock and the bells were supplied by W. Potts and Sons of Leeds who still send someone to check them every six months. The four faces are 5 ft in diameter and the hands are made of copper. The bells were made from various metals by Loughborough bell founders, J. Taylor and Company.

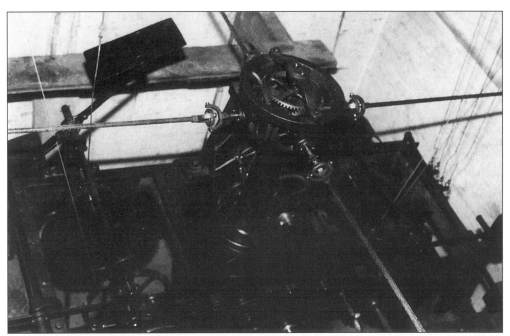

The main cog wheel is 15 inches in diameter; all the faces of the clock are illuminated by electric lights, though originally gas was used.

This clock mechanism has been ticking over for more than a century. The inscription on the brass plate reads, 'This clock and bells were presented to the Borough of Hyde by Joshua Bradley of Godley, cotton mills manager, and was duly started and turned over to the corporation on this day 18 October 1884'. The price was £500. There was a parade from the Town Hall to the Bradley's house where they turned around to the strains of *Auld Lang Syne*. They then made their way back through the flag-decked streets.

Sitting in her carriage outside Aspland House is Mrs Aspland and her grand-daughter Margaret. The coachman was a Mr Richard Preece.

The Town Hall in the early 1900s. To the left is the fire station and to the right, Greenfield Mill. Around the hall is a small wall topped by railings. The time is 9.20 am and it is possibly a Sunday as there are not many folk about.

F.W.SMITH   THE TOWN HALL, HYDE.

Three
Trade

Grandad Brooke stands outside his famous ironmongers in Market Street in the early 1900s. His varied merchandise is displayed on the pavement, on the walls and in the windows upstairs and downstairs, which were illuminated by gas lamps that hung outside them. In 1900 his four children went out for a drive with their governess when the pony slipped, smashing the shafts and pitching the occupants out. Fortunately no one was hurt.

Jack Masser and James Hall, master builders and contractors. They traded as builders from the late 1920s until the early years of the Second World War, constructing many of the houses on Dowson Road. Contracts also took them to North Wales. The photograph was taken during the construction of Cherry Tree Estate, Romily, and they also worked on the Bredbury housing scheme. During the war years they undertook several contracts for the Local Authority, principally erecting public air raid shelters and other defence works.

Mr Albert Knowles, President of the Hairdresser's Union for Hyde and District. He lived in John Street.

Barry Lewis and his grandad in Talbot Road, where the latter had the fish and chip shop opposite St Mary's School. Grandad would go to the fish market in Manchester at about 6.00 am, return, prepare the fish and chips, have a nap, open up the shop at lunch time, not shutting it until 12.00 midnight. During the Second World War when fish was scarce he made his own recipe for 'fish' by boiling up rice until it was very tender then pummelling it, shaping it and putting it in batter.

Ashton Brothers' Works Committee at the main office in 1957.

Tea break at Redferns. Back row, from left to right: Harry Stafford, Phillip Middleton, Harry Critchley, Garnet Redfern, Albert Richardson. Front row: John Phillips, Harold Davis, Sam Ellison, Harold Simpson, Tommy Wilkinson and Frank Laxton.

Some of Redferns work force. Front row, from left to right: Doris Kirkham, Harold Simpson, Bert Henthorn. Second row: Ivy Higginbotham, Nellie Wilde, Lily Etchells, Marion Pannel. Third row: Joe Moss (manager), Annie Higginbotham, Mary Hough, Mrs Hallworth, Nellie O'Brian, -?-, -?-, Arthur Sidebotham, Dora Watson, Lily Evans (foremistress), -?-, Vera Jackson.

Hyde Lane (Market Street) in the early 1900s, showing the Boys Brigade procession, possibly from the Zion in Gee Cross. Note the old Co-op shop on the corner of Queen Street. The shop on the right sold chamois leathers. The owner bought damaged and discarded chamois, then employed ladies to cut them into serviceable pieces and sew them together. It became a very lucrative business.

The gates of Gee Cross Mill, locked for all time. They were made by Abraham Greenwood's Iron Works in Oldham. Today they still stand, being the entrance to new buildings on the site.

The old bridge over the Peak Forest Canal. This enabled workers from Haughton Green to get to the mills in Gee Cross and for the inhabitants of Gee Cross to get to Haughton Green. At one time the canal was very busy as it moved raw materials in and finished goods out. It was also used to provide a packet boat service, though timing was sometimes erratic due to stops at various 'watering holes' along the way. The bridge was replaced in December 1995.

Labour certificate, issued on 16 October 1884, to certify that Eliza Sumner residing in Hyde on 21 October 1884 was not less than 10 years of age and that she had shown to the 'satisfaction of the local authority for this district to be beneficially and necessarily employed.' It was signed by Samuel Rawsthorne, Clerk to the School Attendance Committee. Her date of birth was 9 February 1872 and she was in the fourth standard when she left school at the age of 12.

Shawcross Street, Gee Cross. At one time Orlando Oldham's Cork Factory, it later became the joiner's yard of the builder Samuel Robinson, who built Hyde Town Hall. Later still it was run by Calico Printers.

The junction of Stockport Road and Mottram Old Road, showing how important the area was for transportation - and it is still very busy today. From this crossroads we are directed to Hyde, Denton, Manchester and Ashton in one direction, Mottram, Barnsley and Sheffield in another and Stockport in the third.

The Co-operative movement thrived in Hyde, as in other towns. Saving up your receipts for your 'divi' was a serious thing. Everything could be bought there from food to coal to funerals. This display in Market Street at the main entrance reminds us of the days of loose collars, when everyone had to help look for father's front and back studs. It was also the time when men wore ties for work, even if they did not have a collar.

An impressive display in Greenfield Street, showing a variety of hats, jackets, trousers and overcoats.

The visit of King George VI and Queen Elizabeth, 17 July 1946, seen here driving down Market Street. To the left is Middleton's music shop, then the radio shop advertising 'Bush', followed by Hibbotson's bread shop where two people are standing on chairs in the doorway, as in the next two shops. Others are watching from an upstairs window.

Hyde gasometer. To the left is Haughton Green and to the right are Fletcher Mill and St Stephen's Church. A Mr Isaac Booth founded the original gas works off Back Lane behind the Globe Inn. His enterprise was very successful and before 1850 he had erected and lit the first gas street lamp in Clarendon Place. The price of gas was 7s (35p) per 1,000 cubic foot.

A local milk cart. The harness of the horse is decorated with flowers so it was possibly May Day. There is one gleaming churn in the back along with three passengers. On the side of the cart 'Hattersley' is written so maybe it was from Hattersley Farm.

Levi Hadfield and friend waiting for the milk train at Hyde station, along with others in the background.

Slack Mill engine horse before 1949. Situated on the corner of Smithy Lane and Lumn Road, the machinery was constructed by Daniel Adamsons of Dukinfield in 1898.

A Dr Nicholson's Dynometer. Made by Schaffer and Buden Berg Limited, who had factories in Manchester, London and Glasgow, it was used in Adamson's Works in 1910 to gauge steel tubes.

A boiler made by Joseph Adamsons and Company awaiting transportation by rail.

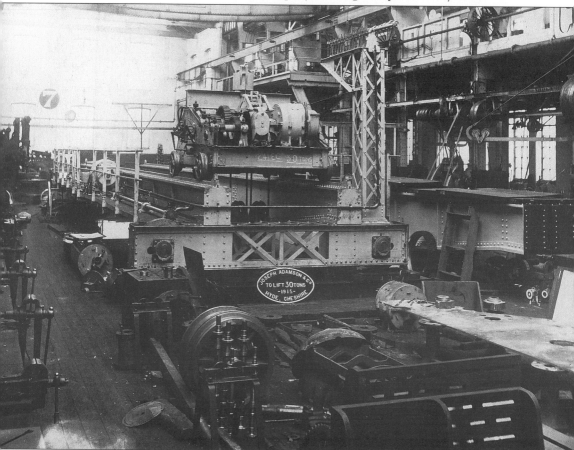

One of the cranes made in 1915 by Joseph Adamsons and Company. It was able to lift 30 tons of material.

Four
Social and Leisure

The Grapes Hotel Bowling Club were the winners of the Hyde and District Amateur Bowling League, 1944/1945. Back row, from left to right: J.S. Gunnell, F. Stanfield, F. Bradbury, W. Hardman, A. Minister, A. Barton, J. Scott, H. Hyde, F. Morris (hon sec). Middle row: J. Shaw, A. Cawley, B. Kelly, W.W. Tuson, J. Masser, H. Harrop (treasurer), F. Shawcross, F. Archer, L. Massey, W. Saxon. Front row: W. Hulme, T. Kershaw, D. Ryan, E. Grist (captain B team), R.B. Kay (president), F. Heywood (chairman), J. Kempster (captain A team), F. Hewitt, A. Knowles and S. Harrison.

The Young Men's Club of St George's are pictured in front of the old school in 1906.

Brownies of St George's. Back row: -?-, Mrs Bocking, -?-, Elizabeth Holmes on the left and Margaret Arnfield on the right; next down on the right side: -?-, Jennifer Leech, -?-, -?-, -?-. Front row: Susan Proctor, -?-, -?-, Joyce Holmes, Gaynor Howcroft, -?-, Jane Booth, -?-, -?-.

Flowery Field Scouts, 1912. John Stone in the centre was the founder of the group and the Scout Master, as well as being the Minister of the Flowery Field Church in 1909. He was born in Bristol in 1880 and educated at Merchant Ventures School where, in 1930, there was a gathering to commemorate the 21st anniversary of his ministry. Tributes were paid to him by Lord Ashton of Hyde, the Mayor and other civic heads of the town.

St George's Cubs marching proudly up Great Norbury Street in the 1950s.

Hyde's first carnival, c. 1928. Back row, from left to right: Harold Greaves, Sam Winterbottom and Mr Winterbottom. Front row: Frank Greaves, William Greaves and Hughie Burgoine. These formed the guard of honour to Randolf Sutton who rode around Hyde in a Co-op milk float. The guards were all staff members of Hyde Theatre, from which they were able to borrow their impressive uniforms.

Production of *The Pirates of Penzance* performed by members of Union Street Methodist Church. On the back row in the centre is Mr G.W. Pickford.

52

The Dandies, 1910, were members of Talbot Road Methodist Church, where they performed concert parties. The members' names were, back row, from left to right: E. Lee, T. Skanny, F. Cartman, J. Greyson, F. Toon, E. Leigh, E. Toon. Sitting down are S. Hudson, -?- and W. Robinson.

The ladies of Talbot Road also participated in giving concerts in the 1940s. Back row, from left to right: M. Howcroft, B. Hadfield, D. Brooks, C. Prest, E. Bennett, A. Connolly. Front row: B. Stanney, E. Robinson, E. Wright, G. Mellor, R. Gaugh, R. Hudson.

St George's Mothers Union with floral tributes after performing one of their splendid plays.

St Stephen's, Newton, 1927. Their operatic society gave a production of Gilbert and Sullivan's *Ruddigore*. In the back row on the left is Alan Green who was the accompanist. Middle row: -?-, Percy Aldcroft, -?-, Percy Grimshaw, Avis Taylor (later Thompson), -?-, -?-. Others named are Herbert Wild, Edith Stanton, Arthur Middleton, Ada Ashton, Mr Gunnel, Harry Cuttle, Mr Blintiss, Bob Smith and Mrs Gunnel.

Eileen Orpitt's dancing class, 1950. All were Gee Cross girls. The eighth dancer from the left on the back row is Margaret Jackson (now Hallas).

Miss Ellison's dancing class performing at the Festival Theatre in March 1957. Second from the left on the back row is Lynn Plant. On the second row, fourth from the left is Eleanor Knott. The kneeling children are, from left to right: Joyce Holmes, Kay Plant, -?-, -?-, -?- and Linda Aplin.

Show time at St George's. The performers were the Mothers Union accompanied by Mrs Thompson's dancing troupe. Next to the back row, seventh from the left is Mrs Adams, on the next row, third from the left is Mrs Harrison, and first on the left in the front row is Mrs Brooks.

Pupils of Bostock dancing class, July 1932. They met at the Parish Rooms at the rear of Edna Street. From left to right: R. Cisley, Irene Marsland, Kathleen Adshead, -?-, -?-, Mary Rhymes, Irene Redfern, -?-.

Hyde Chapel youth in the pantomime *Dick Whittington*, 1952. Back row, from left to right: Leonard Smith, Trevor Truman, -?-, -?-, Beryl Gorrod, Jean Greenhalgh, -?-, -?-. Next row: Hilary Fife, Anne Wood, Jean Gorrod, Jennifer Barber, Pauline Mannion, Margaret Moore, Cora Wilson, Alan Swindels, Marlene Warrington, Margaret Waterworth, Eileen Gorrod, Marjorie Milnes, Vivian Hawley, Margaret Jackson, Ann Stafford, Joan Higgins, -?-, -?-, -?-, -?-, Jocelyn Cooke, Jennifer Hatton, Susan Hopkins, Carole Barton, Pat Patterson, Margaret Patterson. Next row: seventh Brenda or Jean Parker, fourteenth Gregor Mannion, eighteenth David Gorrod, Stuart Bowers (the cat), twenty-sixth Keith Bennison, thirtieth Margaret Dutton; the rest of the names are unknown.

Hilda Ainsworth's dancers performing at the P.S.A. Hall (Pleasant Sunday Afternoon) in 1954. Members include Dorothy Walton, Ann Brierley and Susan Aspin.

Hyde Chapel performance of *Aladdin* in 1949. Back row, from left to right: Eric Downs, Trevor Truman, -?-, -?-, -?-, Anthony Hall, Peggy Kay, Margaret Shelmerdene, Albert Platt. Next row: Christine Pollitt, Margaret Moore, Beryl Gorrod, Joan Stafford, Joyce Baddiley, Andrew Forward, Dorothy Newton, Joan Wimpenny, Nancy Shelmedene, Cyril Morris, Joan Begent, Margaret Higgs, Cora Wilson, Marjorie Bennison. Next row: Marjorie Milnes, Stuart Bowers, Marjorie Pickering, Anne Wood, Jean Gorrod, Marlene Warrington, Margaret Waterworth, Pauline Mannion, Christine Allen, Jennifer Hatton, Hilary Fife, Margaret Jackson, Susan Hopkins, Joan Higgins, -?-, -?-, -?-, Eileen Gorrod, Janet Williams -?-, -?-, -?-, Alan Bramwell. Front row: fourth Miss Greenwood, Sandra Killerley, -?-, -?-, -?-, Pamela Jessop, Margaret Cheetham, Anne Stafford, twenty-first Ann Gonnell, twenty-eighth David Gorrod.

In 1930 Joyce Crighton (née Stanney) and John Ollerenshaw were in the pantomime *Wedding of the Painted Doll*; later they were winners in the Hyde Carnival.

Godley Junior School performed *Jack and the Beanstalk* in December 1979. It was produced by Judith Hill and Barbara Sole. The perfomers were accompanied by the *Godley Grovers* (recorder players) and Mr Frank Doige the headmaster played the piano.

Hyde Historical Society on an outing to Greggs Mill, Styal, July 1986. From left to right: Vanda Fernley, Maureen Stanniforth, Brenda Taylor, Barbara Sole, Norma and Cyril Wood, Ray ?, Eileen Heap.

Husbands and wives return to Hyde after a day trip in the 1920s.

The *clientele* of The Clarendon pub pose for their photograph before embarking on a typical men only outing, all sporting their boaters and buttonholes.

ICI sports day on Walker Lane, 1940s.

Tug of war in the 1960s - ladies versus men perhaps? The ladies are, from left to right, Miss Strong, Cath Greenhalgh and Alma Adams.

In 1920 Alice Hyde won the Leadbitter-Knott cup at the age of 13. She was a keen member of Hyde Seal swimming club.

Members of Hyde Seal club, 1934. Back row: -?-, Alf Hall, Jim Brooks, Jack Bredbury, -?-. The names of those on the front row are unknown.

Hyde Seal swimming club in the old swimming baths in Union Street, 1950s.

VE Day, June 1945, was a time when everyone celebrated victory by having street parties. This one was held in Kew Avenue. Back row, standing: ninth Mrs Dorothy Adamson of Gower Hay, Mrs Ada Ollerenshaw (with baby Susan born on 8 May 1945), twentieth Frank Howcroft, Mrs Jessie Barlow, -?-, Mrs Ellis, Mrs Redfern, Mr Sam Hinchcliffe, Mr Hinchcliffe senior, Mrs Baldwin, Mr Baldwin. Front row of children: -?-, Pat Ellis, -?-, Marjorie Bennison, -?-, -?-, -?-, Alan Baldwin, the rest unknown. There must have been more than one party in the vicinity of Kew Avenue and Kensington Street because many relatives of the people in the picture are missing from it.

Garden party on the lawn of St Thomas's Parsonage, 7 August 1909.

Kathleen Adshead's fourteenth birthday party in 1938. Bottom row, from left to right: Renee Booth, Beryl Wood, Fred Booth, Betty Cooper, Irene Cooper, Hazel Chaplin. Second row: Mary Don, Diana Butler (with kitten), Rosalind Allen, Katheen Adshead, Dorothy Wright, Margaret Cooper. Third row: Lillian Wilde, Jean Bramhall, Elsie Hall, Lilian Hardy, Kathleen Williamson, Irene Bradshaw. Back row: Elsie Moores, Emily Barlow, Alice Cooper and Joyce Booth.

Birthday party for Catherine (5) and Edith (17) Lockett, August 1920. The photograph was taken outside the family home. Top row, from left to right: Watkin Lockett, Mrs Elliot, Florrie Redfern, Arthur Shaw, -?-, Hazel Redfern, Edith Lockett, Ginny Griffiths, Grandma Lockett, Gertie Lockett, Grandad Lockett. Second row: Maggie Robinson, -?-, -?-, -?-, Lizzie Elliot, Doris Dakin, Alice Holt, Emmie Hiskiss, -?-. Bottom row: Harold Wood, Florence Bradshaw, Annie Lockett, Catherine Lockett, Lizzie Redfern, Tommy Bennett, Mary Johnson and May Lockett.

Unknown team in 1912. Front row, from left to right: Mr Hoyne, Mr Davies, -?-, Mr Brereton and Mr Robinson, who may have played for Hyde United.

St Stephen's Sunday School football club, 1909/1910.

The young football players of St George's, 1950/1951. The third chap from the left on the back row is Frank Bowler.

Team members during the season of 1961/1962. Back row, from left to right: Lincoln Delve, Mr Cox, David Garratt. Next row: Bob Pritchard, Alan Higginbotham, Paul Hibbert, Brian Simpson. Front row: Denis Charnock, Greg Mannion, Mike Sutton, Roy Smith, Trevor Leach.

MOTTRAM DEANERY FOOTBALL LEAGUE

CUP FINALS

FRIDAY, 4th MAY, 1962

at BENNETT STREET, HYDE.   Kick-off 6-15 p.m.

Hyde United Supporters' Club Cup
HYDE ST. GEORGES v. UNION ST. CONGS., HYDE

Gillott Cup
HYDE LADS' CLUB v. AUDENSHAW ST. STEPHEN'S

ADMISSION : 9d.   Old Age Pensioners 6d. pay at gate
BUS No. 4 or 4A from Hyde Bus Station.

Cup Final ticket for the Mottram Deanery Football League, Friday 4 May 1962. Admission cost 9d (3½p); old age pensioners 6d (2½p). The ground could be reached by taking a No. 4 or 4A bus from Hyde bus station.

Players in the late 1960s. Back row, from left to right: Ken Fernley, Dave Jenkins, Phil Bailey, David Garratt, Michael Monton, Terrence Banks, Peter ?, Alan Cook. Front row: Mike Wrigley, -?-, Harry Jack, Barry Ponten, Arthur Chesworth.

St George's football team in the Stockport Sunday School League. Back row, from left to right: Alan Crook, Fred Garratt, John Hilton, David Garratt, Peter Bailey, Ian Firth, Mick Morton, Ken Fernley. Front row: Dave Jenkins, Barry Porter, Harry Jack, Duncan Haddow, Mike Wrigley.

Greenfield Street athletics team in the 1960s. Back row, from left to right: Mr Howse, Kenny Saville, Trevor Leach, David Prout, Barry Walsh, ? Saville, ? Roberts, Paul Hibbert, Mr Cox. Front row: Bob Pritchard, David Garratt, Howard Gee, Malcolm Sutton, Lincoln Delve, Ian Heywood, -?-.

Unknown football club but possibly that of Holy Trinity. Back row, from left to right: -?-, Mary Russell, Joe Mellor, Denis Taylor, Norman Walker, Dorothy Mellor, Gordon Jackson, Harry Dilkes, Laura Wilson, Leslie Barton, Winnie ?, Charlie Perrin, Doreen Hampson, Ethel Wilson, Peggy Russell. Middle row, sitting: C. Hyde, Tom Hill, Gordon Mellor, Arnold Hill, Jack Sparks. Front row: Tom Russell, Alf Daniels, Tom Townsend, Sam Palmer, Tony Metcalf, Ronnie ? and John Fleming holding the ball.

St George's cricket team, 1949. Back row, from left to right: George Ingham, Bill Allott, David Lees, John Smith and Mr Ratcliffe. Next row: Frank Alexander, Alan Hampson, Victor Vernon, ? Bucher, Alan Rothwell. Front row: Barry Kent, Bill Bardsley, Billy Hadfield, Ian Firth, John Robinson, Tony McConnell and Frank Bowler.

Hyde's old cricket team, suitably attired in their 'whites'.

Local caddies on Werneth Low, June 1911.

Venus the dog was well known along Mottram Old Road. He was bred by Mr M.W. Beven of Mottram and owned by Mr Knowles of Hyde, who was a hairdresser.

Barry Lewis, who once lived in Talbot Road and now lives in Australia, is seen here getting to grips with his tricycle. Behind him is his grandad's fish and chip shop.

Zion's Cadet band sporting their various certificates for music.

Five

Celebrations

Whitsuntide procession. The young pupils of Holy Trinity, Gee Cross, are walking down Stockport Road.

A wedding in the early 1900s. The boy in the centre of the group is Jack Holmes.

Possibly a church function around the turn of the century.

Peace celebrations in 1920. On the front row on the right hand side is Alice Hyde.

St George's Sunday School banner in the 1960s. Jim Kerfoot and Mr E. Holmes are carrying it one Whitsuntide. They have just passed the Theatre Royal on Corporation Street. The young ladies are dressed in the very fashionable mini skirts of the time.

St George's Whit Walk, 1956. The gentleman in front of the man with the hat on is Jim Kerfoot. The two gents on the left are twins, Geoff and Derek Booth, who were solicitors in Hyde.

St George's Mothers Union passing along Higher Henry Street, Whitsuntide 1956. Note that all the ladies are wearing hats. Mrs Weker, Mrs Adams, Mrs Docker, Mrs Bancroft and Mrs Wilde are some of the members.

Central Methodist Church during their Whit procession on Market Street in 1941. In the foreground is Edith Pimlott, who at this time was the leader of the primary department.

Julie Robinson and Julie Adams patiently waiting to set off on a St George's Whit Walk in the 1950s.

Hoviley Methodist Church with umbrellas at the ready during a wet Whit Week in 1953. The gentleman in the centre is Mr Taylor.

St George's Mothers Union all kitted out for the wet weather. The hoardings show adverts for electricity, milk, gas, bread and the famous speedway at Belle Vue.

A large group of men from St Paul's, Godley, at Whitsun, passing the Town Hall, all suitably attired in suits, overcoats and hats.

Young ladies from St Thomas's Church all dressed in their finery at a Whitsun in the 1920s. Many wear high buttoned boots and all have beautifully decorated hats.

The 1979 Whit Sunday Walk by the Central Methodist Church just passing the bus shelter opposite the Town Hall. Walking under the banner is Mr Crighton who was the Sunday School Superintendent at that time. In front of the procession are Eric Crossley, Reverend B. Redhead and John Charlton.

The little ones outside Pole Bank on Whit Friday, 1951. The lady in the centre is Gladys Lockyear (now King). She is holding hands with Brenda Nield and Margaret Ryan.

Tiny tots with their cotton, floppy, mop caps walk in between the tram lines at Whitsuntide. The adult in the centre is Edith Booth (née Hyde) with her daughter Ivy (later Galvin).

St George's Sunday School ready for the Whit Walk in 1954. The young men are standing outside the old school wearing their distinctive ties. On the left of the group is Eric Holmes who later became a butcher on Croft Street.

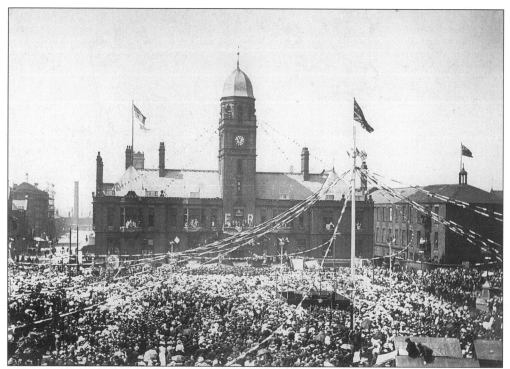

The people of Hyde gathering together in the Market Square in 1902 to celebrate the coronation of King Edward VII. To the left of the hall is Greenfield Mill. In the foreground to the right a couple of boys have climbed onto the roofs of the permanent market stalls.

The Duke of Gloucester unveils the plaque at the official opening of the Country Park.

82

Miss Alma Adams standing in front of the bonfire built on Werneth Low in 1939. It was built in the field to the left of the grass triangle. Notice the precision of the wood stacking and the smattering of snow around its base.

Tintwhistle Band playing at Godley Water Works' open day, July 1986.

St Andrew's Church in John Street. The altar is decorated with daffodils so it is probably Easter time. The minister was the Reverend Broadbent.

Artist Meet, celebrating Christmas at Central Methodist Church. Back row, from left to right: Jean Hall, Win Robinson, Margaret Harwood, Kathleen Adams, Alan Taylor, Ray Howard, Joan Jackson, Isolde Blurton, Hamish Lennox, Barbara Johnson, Dorothy Lomas, Doreen Hiller, Kathleen Herod. Front row: Madge Briggs, Netta Addy, Gladys Grantham, Gladys Cook, Moira Hares, Barbara Sole and Sylvia Main.

Returning from the service held in Hyde Park to celebrate the coronation of Queen Elizabeth II in 1953. From the front are, B. Stanney, E. Bennett, A. Connolly, G. Lees, B. Hadfield, D. Brooks, Mrs Hardman and R. Hudson. They are walking down Talbot Road with their umbrellas at the ready.

The unveiling of the plaque at the Country Park by the Aspland family and the last of the young people to be born at Asplands Maternity Home. The gate post behind them was transferred by the Loxley Building Company after the demolition of the maternity home. Part of the inscription reads: 'These pillars came from Werneth Lodge, the nearby home of the Aspland family, given by them in perpetuity to the people of Hyde. To be used for the benefit of the children and converted into Asplands Maternity Hospital.'

Alfred Johnson dressed as a cardinal for the Whit procession with St Paul's of Godley.

The carter from J. Ashtons and Company, Newton Mills, between 1920 and 1930. The horse is all decked out with flowers so it is possibly a May Day.

The return of St George's Church bells on 14 August 1920 after their re-casting by Messrs Taylor and Company of Loughborough at a cost of £1,400. John Chadwick and Sons, of 69 Nelson Street, was the carrier of these two particular bells. There was a procession through the town headed by the Borough Band to welcome the bells home.

The first May Queen for the crowning of the statues at St Paul's, Godley, in 1910. The Queen was Miss Quinn.

The Central Methodist Sunday School in George Street held the crowning of the Rose Queen in the Sunday School in 1940. The retiring Rose Queen was Margaret Dickenson; her successor was Marjorie Thompson. Back row, from left to right: Barbara Hampson, Ethel McGee, Margaret Dickenson, Marjorie Thompson, -?-, Joan Baker. Next row: Margaret Cullen, Jean Haugh, Doreen Moss, -?-. Front row: Nellie Cullen, -?-, Irvine Hulme, ? Thompson, Stuart Holden, Derek Haugh, Squire Bennett, -?-.

The crowning of Miss Marjorie Alwyn Bennison of Stockport Road, Gee Cross, as May Queen of Hyde Chapel in 1950. The retiring Queen was Joan Wimpenny. From the left are: Marjorie Bennison, Barbara Thornley and Margaret Jackson; Heather Richards and Elizabeth Badeley were train bearers.

The crowning of the Rose Queen at Hyde Baptist Church, c. 1930. Back row, from left to right: Hettie Davis, Nellie France (the Queen), Madge Mottram. Next row: Gordon Roland, Ada Saville, Muriel Roland, Margaret Welch, Jean Mellor, Donald Hudson, Lily Lawton; May Naish and John Barnes are sitting.

Betty Oldham was crowned May Queen at Leigh Street School on 6 May 1939. Back row, from left to right: Sybil Day, -?-, J. Oldham, Betty Oldham, Doreen Simpson (retiring Queen), May Naish, Margaret Ollerenshaw, Betty France. The young ladies kneeling are Miss Higginbotham, Miss Whitworth, June Day and Cathleen Ogden.

The May Queen at St Paul's, Godley. Cathleen Smith is the little girl on the left of the Queen.

Flowery Field's May Queen, 1943. Left, Marion Cooper (Queen), -?-, Celia Armitage, Irene Stubbs and Polly Brooks.

The crowning of the Hyde Chapel Rose
Queen in 1953. The new Queen was Ruth
Water and the retiring one, Margaret Moore.

On the left is Polly Brooks, the retiring
Queen in 1943. Marion Wagstaff is on the
right.

Hyde Chapel Rose Queen, 1952. Left to right: Margaret Cheetham, Pamela Jessop, -?-, Heather Badley, Anne Stafford, David Platt, Keith Bennison, Margaret Moore, Margaret Jackson.

The celebration of the Golden Wedding of Sarah and Harper Jackson in 1957.

The wedding of Cyril Jackson and Winnie Quirk.

Mr and Mrs William Lewis's wedding group during the Second World War.

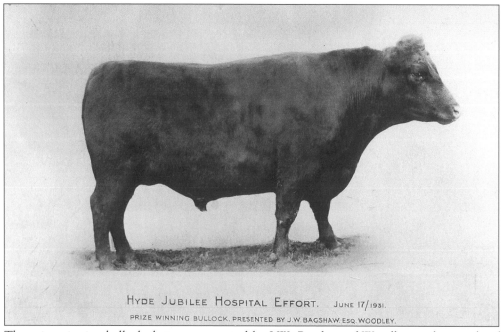

HYDE JUBILEE HOSPITAL EFFORT. JUNE 17/1931.

PRIZE WINNING BULLOCK. PRESENTED BY J.W. BAGSHAW. ESQ. WOODLEY.

The prize-winning bullock that was presented by J.W. Bagshaw of Woodley to the people of Hyde for the Jubilee celebrations on 17 June 1931.

Christmas time in the 1950s. The children of Redferns employees gather for a good time.

Six

Institutions

Gee Cross Council School, 1934. Back row, from left to right: Harry Denerley, Eric Lyne, Raymond Molesdale. Third row: Edna Horsfield, Freda Knott, Norma Barry, Vera Nelson, Kathleen Sherwin, John Harding, Jim Bagshaw, Tom O'Sullivan, Harold Saxton. Second row: Betty Shelmerdine, Margaret Knowles, Margaret Wilde, Jean Bramhall, Mary Wilcocks, Betty Denerley. Front row: George Yates, Dudley Luke, Raymond Masser, George Jackson, George Harrison, Lesley Whitehead, Tony Metcalfe.

The Hyde branch of the W.E.A. (Workers Education Association) on holiday in Ammerdown, near Bath, in 1986. Back row, from left to right: Alice Parkey, Betty McEown, Mildred Ireland, Florence Berry, Joan Flood. Middle row: Edna Milnes and Barbara Wilde. Nora Edwards is at the front.

Hyde Historical Society at Styal Mill in 1986. Back row, from left to right: -?-, Doreen Knight, Kathleen Adams, Vanda Fernley, -?-, Maureen ?, Cyril Wood. Front row: Betty Makey, Eileen Heap, Barbara Sole, Brenda Taylor, Norma Wood, Ray ?.

Reverend Shaw from Waterhead giving a talk on local dialect at Beely Street Centre, 2 March 1987. Back row, from left to right: Marie Quinn, Betty Maley, -?-, Charles Atkinson, -?-, Hilda Hibbert, -?-, Vanda Fernley, Kathleen Adams. Front row: Brenda Taylor, Reverend Shaw, Les Taylor.

Hyde Cub's Gang Show, at the Festival Theatre, Christmas 1970. John Walton, Rodger Elly, Andrew Elly, Andrew Hallas, Andrew Neil, Geoffrey Lloyd, Nigel Whittingslow and Neil Rutherford were among the performers.

Some of St George's Scouts and families during wartime. Back row, from left to right: Mr Boot, Les Tongue, David Adams, Derek Carter. Middle row: Mrs Boot and Mrs Tongue. Front row: two sons of Mr and Mrs Boot and the son of Mr and Mrs Tongue.

St George's Cubs in the church grounds in the 1950s. On the right of the Cub Mistress is Frank Oldham.

The 7th Hyde Guides and Brownies posed on Talbot Road for this picture in the 1930s. The minister was the Revd G. Strangroom. The seated Guide officials are Amy Robinson, Margaret Robinson, Blanche Garside and Amy Wilde. The men who are sitting are the Sunday School Superintendents: Jim Bedford and Thomas Stanney. The second Brownie from the left is Joyce Stanney.

The 1st Newton Scout Troop posed for this photograph on Talbot Road in the 1930s.

The 5th Hyde Scout Troop. On the back row at the far right is Tom Bromley.

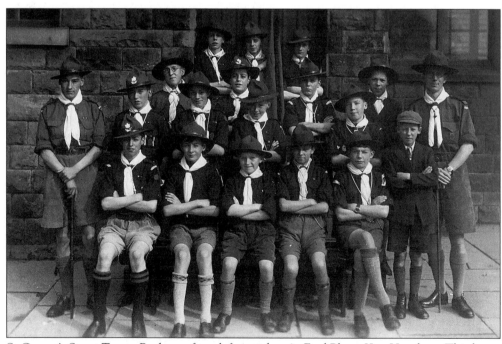

St George's Scout Troop. Back row from left to right: -?-, Fred Plant, Ken Henshaw. Third row: -?-, Roy Davis, Will Booth. Second row: Martin ?, Lawrence Samuels, Jack Brooda, David Adams, Jack Renshaw, Johnny Clark. Front row: Norman Harrison, Jack Lloyd, Neville Jones, Frank Cook.

Hyde Salvation Army in 1927. The Andrew sisters are in the middle of the front row. Miss Ethel May at the right end of the middle row was the aunt of Edith Pimlott.

Albert Knowles on the left won the Military Cross in the First World War. As a young man he was a member of the Harriers and as a child he was well known for the speed at which he could run. He lived at the top cottages on Joel Lane and if a candle was needed in a hurry he would run down to the village and back in a matter of minutes. During the war it was his swiftness of foot which saved his comrades from death.

The first war cortege in Hyde in 1916 was for the funeral of Elijah Smith.

Outside St George's Elijah's regiment salute him.

St George's Church Lads Brigade, 1912. Second from the left with the rifle is Fred Robinson. From their stance one would think that they were preparing for war.

George Street Boys Brigade, 1st Hyde Company, in the 1930s.

These well dressed men were the bell ringers at St George's Church. Back row, from left to right: -?-, -?-, Mr Howcroft, Bill Norgrove, -?-, -?-, and Tom Wilde, who for a time worked at Ardens as the foreman. During the First World War the bells remained silent, only being rung to celebrate its end.

Zion men's class. Second from the left is Ernest Hyde.

Men's Bible class at Holy Trinity. Back row, from left to right: Mr Growcott (headmaster), Fred Gee, Teddy Harrison, Denis Ogden, Len Turner, Leslie Armitage, Tommy Memody, Canon Richmond. Front row: Mr Thatcher, then the names are unknown until Arnold Hill, who is at the end.

Gee Cross Council School in Enfield Street in 1949. Back row, from left to right: Miss Lucas, Pat Wright, Ann Swindells, Pauline Squires, Marjorie Pickering, Bernice Wipp, Margaret Mann, Margaret Jackson, June Higginbotham, Joan ?, Miss Wood (headmistress). Third row: Judith Grimshaw, Alan Hill, Norman Slater, Rodger Dickenson, David Langtry, Brian Howarth, Kathleen Stafford. Second row: Janet Williams, Norma Chanley, Dorothy Oldham, Christine ?, Pat Paterson, Irene Hadley, Mavis Clitheroe. Front row: Peter Wagstaff, David Higgins, John Oldham, David Carrol, Ronnie Birtles and Gordon Clarke.

St George's Class V. Back row, from left to right: Miss Wood, Mr Birch, the headmaster at the right. Middle row: sixth Margaret Archer, seventh Dorothy Hopwood. Front row: Frank Bowler, seventh Beryl Downhill and Bill Allott at the end.

St George's Class VI, 1931. On the far right of the second row is Mr Wood the headmaster. Second from the left on the front row is Sidney Robinson, fifth Wilf Stringer and eighth Jesse Lowe.

George Street British School, 1906. The headmaster was Mr Edge. A lot of the children are wearing lacy collars which were for decoration rather than necessity. Many families were very poor and not every child had a best outfit so the photographers would carry such collars around with them; sometimes they would only be paper doilies.

Flowery Field Infant School in the 1900s. Third from the back on the left is George Holmes.

Hyde Grammar School was opened in Edna Street in 1877. This is the original desk of the headmaster. The telephone has been in use for over fifty years and was still functioning in 1982.

The coat hooks on the walls of the first Hyde Grammar School are now used for the storage of various tools and patterns.

Mr Booth's class at St George's day school, September 1958. Back row, from left to right: -?-, -?-, Graham Whittaker, Derek Wadsworth, -?-, Michael Greaves, -?-, Philip Saxon. Second row: -?-, Kay Plant, Linda Perrie, Audrey Plant, Susan Oldham, Denise Underhill, -?-, Caroline Freeman. Front row: Heather Henderson, Dorothy Taylor, Gillian Skirven, -?-, -?-, Sylvia Smith, Vivienne Mason, Joyce Holmes, -?-, -?-.

St Mary's Primary School, 1955. Back row, from left to right: Trevor Nixon, David Sowter, Steven Moore, Ian Bradbury, Peter Rowlands, Gordon Hogg, Barry Lewis, Maurice Barlow. Fourth row: Mrs Clegg, Graham Dootson, Ann ?, Janice Worthington, Erica Seddon, Judith ?, Ann Burgess, -?-, -?-, Colin Turner, Mrs Kinleyside. Third row: John Heywood, Joyce Hewitt, Anne Clegg, Brenda Clarke, Janice Smith, -?-, Ann Howcroft, Valerie Linney, Carol Holt, Susan Norton, Brian Blenkinsop. Second row: Jean Adshead, Carol ?, Susan Gerrard, -?-, Sandra Tatton, -?-, Christine Adshead, -?-, Rita Shuttleworth. Front row: Kevin Pentney, Frank Wright, Eric Whittaker, Stanley Mills, Eric Delaney, Eric Hilton, Patrick ?, David Gibson, Michael Shuttleworth.

The last year of Standard III, George Street Council School, October 1928. The group of five girls on the left are Mary Bocking, Lena Harrison, Lydia Mather, Kate Booth, -?-. Back row, from left to right: Henry Shepley, Harold Samuels, Harry Stafford, John Hindley, ? Burgess, Tom Grant, Albert Gee, Miss Myers, Mr Lincoln the headmaster. Fourth row: Tom Cree, Tom Wigley, Clarence Newton, Herbert Fell, -?-, -?-, ? Dale. Third row: Edith Allott, Ada ?, May Cree, Alice Lomas, ? Brown, Liza Feltcher, -?-, George Holt. Second row: Mary Parker, Annie Garet, Hilda Sumner, Dora Dale, Beatrice Hudson, Alice Taylor, -?-, Doris Holt, -?-. Front row: Elizabeth Bray, -?-, Irene Bray, -?-, Irene Partington, -?-, Marion Braddock, Margaret Hallas, Gladys Wood, Nellie Bynion, Ralph Wright.

St George's School, 1938. Back row, from left to right: Miss Dykes, -?-, -?-, Edith Cheetham, Esther Crowley, -?-, -?-. Third row: John Dolan, Irene Hamer, -?-, -?-, ? Townsend, Nelly Tucker, Anthony Browning, Vera Smith, -?-, ? Worthington. Second row: -?-, -?-, ? Lawler, -?-, Edith Robinson, Herbert Perry, Doris Greenwood, -?-, -?-, -?-. Front row: -?-, ? Mackenzie, -?-, -?-, Ernest Oliver, -?-, Joyce Leah, Eric Winston, -?-, -?-.

St George's School, Class IV, 1931. Back row, from left to right: Ron Nash, Maurice Christopher, John Day, Fred Plant, -?-, -?-, -?-, ? Wilde, -?-, John Morris. Fifth row: Evelyn Myatt, Nancy Howett, Marjorie Hartley, -?-, -?-, Barbara Wadsworth, Joan Richardson, Alice Barnes, Beryl Knowles. Fourth row: Miss Dyke, Moira Greaves, Nancy Beal, -?-, -?-, Alma Adams, -?-, -?-, -?-, -?-, Mr Wood the headmaster. Third row: sixth Cicily Walker, Lily Broadbent. Second row: Roy Davies, Richmond Harvey, rest unknown. Front row: all unknown.

Leigh School in the late 1920s. The young lady on the far right of the back row is Rose Hannah Lowe (later Kerfoot).

The beginners department at Central Methodist Sunday School in 1957; Mrs Edith Pimlott was the leader.

Holy Trinity infant department, 1923. Back row, from left to right: Miss Coupe, Miss Emmerson. Second row: -?-, S. Brian, ? Cooper, -?-, -?-, -?-, A. Searle, H, Jackson, -?-, -?-. Front row: J. Shaw, -?-, -?-, L. Downhill, S. Greenhalgh, A. Daniels, rest unknown

Holy Trinity School, 1927. Back row, from left to right: -?-, S. Brian, -?-, A. Mellor. Third row: Mr Growcott, T. Noden, T. Booth, S. Greenhalgh, J. Mellor, E. Thompson, Miss Nuttall. Second row: H. Jackson, T. Russell, F. Schofield, -?-, J. King. Front row: S. Marsland, J. Forder, A. Searle.

Holy Trinity sports day on Werneth Low in 1906. The headmaster Mr Bowker stands ready to blow the whistle to start the girl's skipping race.

Borough of Hyde Education Committee.

TOTAL EXEMPTION CERTIFICATE.

Education Act. 1921.   Sections 42 and 138 (1).

I CERTIFY that _Harry Lever_

residing at _12 Gair St, Hyde_

according to particulars given in the Certificate of Birth produced to me reached the age of

Fourteen years on the _18th_ day of _November_ 19 37

and is exempt from attendance at school on and after the _23rd_ day

of _December_ 19 37 .

Signed _H V Lightfoot_

Secretary for Education.

Dated this _23rd_ day of _December_ 19 37 .

1 000/4/36.   H.P.CO.—T13606.

The Total Exemption Certificate, Education Act 1921, Sections 42 and 138. When young people left school to find work at the age of 14, legally they should have had this type of certificate. It reads: 'I certify that Harry Lever, residing at 12 Gair Street, Hyde, according to particulars given in the certificate of birth, produced to me, reached the age of 14 years on 18 day of November 1937, and is exempt from attendance at school on and after the 23 day of December 1937. Signed H.V. Lightfoot, Secretary for Education.'

In the early 1900s great store was set by making people aware of the dangers of alcohol abuse. Lectures were given at schools and each pupil had to write a short essay on the abuse of drink. If the essay was acceptable they were given a certificate like this one, awarded to Sam Crumbie. It says 'Certificate of Merit awarded under the Schools Scientific Temperance Teaching Scheme of the Lancashire and Cheshire Band of Hope and Temperance Union.'

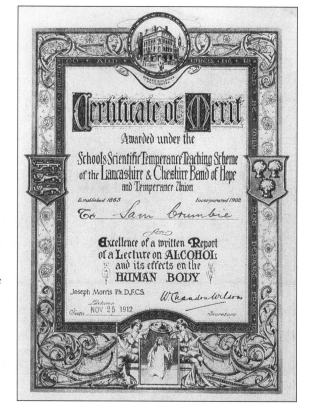

Seven

People of Hyde

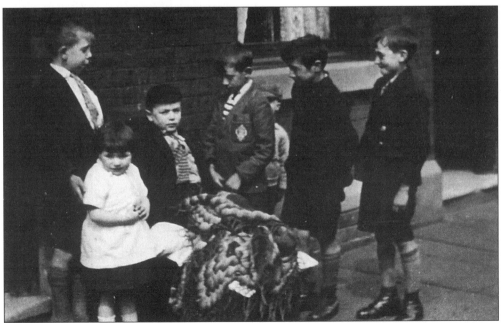

Albion Street, 1932. From left to right: Annie Broadbent, Tom Wilde with his broken leg, Sydney Scholes, Harold Robinson and Lawrence Ridgeway.

Florrie Lowe and Mary Jane who lived in Foundry Street, which used to run from Crook Street to the top of Hovily Brow. Florrie, on the left, is wearing iron tipped clogs and Mary Jane has high buttoned boots.

Cathleen Smith of Godley, dressed in her finery after attending the crowning of the May Queen at St Paul's Church.

Harrry Lever sits in the side car and Fred Lever is all set to take him for a ride. The bike and side car were won in a Christmas raffle in 1929 at Hornby's Bazaar on Hyde Lane, now Market Street. Mrs Lever was the lady who had the winning ticket.

Kate and Maria Holmes. Kate married Arthur Booth and was the mother of twins Geoff and Derek, who later became local solicitors.

The brother and sister who married a brother and sister. From the left, Arnold Booth and Annie Cooper; Jim Cooper and Winnie Booth. The photograph was taken during the First World War. Jim was the owner of the family butchers on Bennett Street, near The Cheshire Cheese in Newton.

Mr James Crumbie and his wife Eliza Ann sit in front of their children, James, Alice, Samuel, Mary Jane and Ada. The family lived in Gair Street, Flowery Field.

Jesse Baddeley and family near their home in
Gower Hey Wood, Gee Cross.

Norma Wood, the first secretary of the
Hyde Historical Society and Brenda
Taylor, the founder and first chairman.

The Ollerenshaw family in 1915. At the back is Private William Ollerenshaw of the 21st Battalion of the Manchester Regiment. In the foreground are his parents, William and Harriet, and his younger brother Harold. William junior was killed in action in France on 25 March 1917, aged 20. The family lived in Kensington Street.

The Cooper family, *c.* 1911-12, who resided in Meadow Avenue. Back row, from left to right: Jim, Ida, Ethel, William, Maria, Ann. Second row: George and Joe. Front row: George (father), grandmother, Hilda and mother.

John Oldham, who was an expert in folk legends and a founder member of Stockport Heritage. In the 1950s and '60s he worked at Denton Library where he started the gramophone section. He lived most of his life in Gee Cross where he was a Unitarian youth leader with Hyde Chapel. He took a leading role in Hyde Action Group's fight against developers and council officials to save Werneth Low as a haven for the public. His action and that of others led directly to the founding of Werneth Country Park, a trust land which was bought by the people of Hyde but on which developers tried to build in the 1970s.

Samuel Robinson, who was born in 1827 and died in 1893, was the second son of Joseph Robinson who was born at Litton, near Tideswell, Derby, in 1803. His mother Alice was born in Werneth in 1800. Samuel was one of the main contractors for the building of the Town Hall.

Private Walter Isherwood (later sergeant) of the Lancashire Fusiliers. He won the DCM on 9 October 1917 at Passchendale.

Harry Lever at the age of 1 in 1924. During his working life he picked up several nicknames, one of which was 'Hatbox' Harry. He worked on the railways for 34 years, having started as an oiler and greaser and then becoming a wagon repairer. He worked at Ardwick West and Mottram yard and checked wagons for the Woodhead line freights. Later he became an examiner and a rolling stock technician. The name 'Hatbox' came about because in one shift he found eighty-four hot axle boxes in 8 hours. Crews from Sheffield and Rotherwood knew him as the 'Whistling Tapper' because as he worked he could whistle classical tunes. Other nicknames were 'Electric Lips' and 'Budgie'. He has a great fondness for history, especially about Hyde.

Mr and Mrs William Davis. Mrs Davis was called Phoebe and was well known in Hyde as the lady who worked in Hulme's tripe hut in the market. Bill worked for Hyde Corporation on a lorry that cleaned the grids with a long tube. Phoebe came originally from Nottingham where her father was a Police Chief Constable.

Six of Hyde's prettiest girls as they appeared in the final of the Festival Queen beauty competition. From left to right: Doreen Topley, Marion Hunt, Alwyn Smith (winner), Mildred Rickson, May Ashton and Maureen Dykings.

Mr T.H. Cumberlidge who was one of the presidents of Hyde Lads Club.

Alderman Breakey, Mayor of Hyde in Coronation year, 1953.

Canon Mars of St Paul's, Godley, was a very friendly and approachable man, willing to help any even if they did not belong to his church. He was a great friend of J.V.A. Danby, the first Chief Constable of Hyde.

The Reverend Theobald and his wife.

Local amateur artist John Slater, from Newton. He has painted many local scenes but his great love is the Lake District.

Mr Arthur Garland, a prolific painter of all subjects, lived in Werneth Low.

Manchester-born Charles Smith worked as a railway man after leaving the army in 1948. He began painting in 1981 and within a year held his first exhibition. In 1987 he left his job as a train driver to concentrate on his painting and now spends much of his time at Werneth Low, a subject he has painted many times.

Trevor Grimshaw, who was born in Hyde in 1947 and studied at Stockport College of Art from 1963-67. He has had numerous one man exhibitions in this country and abroad. Trevor's powerful industrial landscapes focus on the familiar scenes of North West mill towns in decline and transform them into disturbing, moving images.

Ivy Naish, 1919.

Barbara Jean Barber in 1944, with her
doll which came all the way from
Belgium during the Second World War.